Brimming with creative inspiration, how-to projects, and useful information to enrich your everyday life, quarto.com is a favorite destination for those pursuing their interests and passions.

World of Weird © 2022 Quarto Publishing plc.
Text © 2022 Tom Adams
Illustrations © 2022 Celsius Pictor

First Published in 2022 by Wide Eyed Editions,
an imprint of The Quarto Group.
100 Cummings Center, Suite 265D, Beverly, MA 01915 USA.
T +1 978-282-9590 F +1 978-283-2742 **www.Quarto.com**

A catalogue record for this book is available from the British Library.

ISBN 978-0-7112-6954-5

The illustrations were created digitally
Set in Remington Noiseless and Mrs Eaves

Published by Georgia Amson-Bradshaw
Edited by Hattie Grylls
Art Direction by Hanri van Wyk
Design Assistance by Lyli Feng
Production by Dawn Cameron

Manufactured in Guandong, China TT052022
9 8 7 6 5 4 3 2 1

Illustrations reproduced by kind permission of: Alamy Stock Photo: 13, 27t, 32b, 36t; Boscastle Museum of Witchcraft: 51b; istockphoto: 33t; National Portrait Gallery: 23; Science Photo Library: 43; Shutterstock: 49, throughout; The Mary Evans Picture Library: 58; Wikimedia Commons: 22t, 22b, 26t, 26b, 28r, 34b, 46, 56b.

Every effort has been made to identify or trace copyright holders of material reproduced in this book. The publisher would be pleased to rectify any omissions in subsequent editions.

WORLD OF WEIRD

A Creepy Compendium of True Stories

By
Dr. McCreebor

Written by
Tom Adams

Illustrated by
Celsius Pictor

CONTENTS

Dear Reader,

Welcome to Dr. McCreebor's *World of Weird*, a creepier collection of the odd and eccentric you couldn't wish to find. Firstly, let me introduce myself. I'm Dr. Leila McCreebor, great-granddaughter of the eminent explorer and philosopher Dr. McCreebor. I must confess, I'd not even heard of my long-dead great-granddaddy until, while clearing out the attic in the family home, I came across an old crate of notebooks and manuscripts belonging to him.

One look at the papers and I realized why my family had failed to mention the good doctor. Ma and Pa were quite straitlaced, and it looks like Dr. M was anything but. He was an odd fish and so the McCreebor clan were keen to expurgate him from the family tree. Thankfully, these papers appear to have slipped through the net, and once I started looking through them, I knew I had to share them with a wider audience.

You see, my great-grandfather loved the bizarre. The more mysterious or gruesome the better!

So, what is contained in the manuscripts?

McCreebor lived during the reign of Queen Victoria, a time when the world was opening up, with more and more people exploring the globe. This kick-started a mania for collecting and cataloguing. Great-gramps, like many, wanted to find out about the world, to understand how nature worked, and to figure out the laws of science in the hope of making sense of our time on Earth.

The wealthy and well-educated aspired to owning a cabinet of curiosities, a display of interesting knickknacks they'd collected on their expeditions. These cabinets were found in palaces and stately homes across Europe and their owners believed they revealed just how well-traveled and intelligent they were.

The curios were classified into groups, each given a name in Latin: pieces of art (*artificialia*), natural objects, animals, and people (*naturalia*), and scientific instruments (*scientifica*). The doctor, being a lover of oddity, added extra categories for the things that particularly took his fancy: crime and punishment (*scelus et supplicium*), the spirit world (*spiritualis*), magic (*magicae*), and death (*morteum*).

While many that toured the globe helped themselves to whatever objects they liked, I'm proud to say that Dr. McCreebor did things differently. He journeyed carefully, respectfully, and with sensitivity. He listened and observed, always on the lookout for that elusive object that might, or might not, exist. However, he'd never take these objects home. He knew these pieces weren't his to possess. Instead, he recorded everything in his notebooks, writing about and sketching the treasures he came across. These notebooks are his cabinet of curiosities.

In some instances, when I think the doctor has misunderstood something, I've added my own comments. He was very trusting and tended to believe all he was told. I take more of a scientific approach.

But his papers remain fascinating reading. I hope you think so too.

Enjoy.

Dr. Leila McCreebor

*When you see this writing...
it's me!*

GALILEO'S FINGER

The blood of Christ is an astonishing find. But, in an ancient library in Florence, Italy, is another relic. This one though is not religious, but scientific. It's the bony finger of one of the greatest scientists ever.

The Italian astronomer Galileo Galilei, who died in 1642, is known as the father of modern science. One hundred years after his death his body was moved to a grander tomb and, in the move, some body parts went missing—two fingers, a thumb, a vertebra, and a tooth. Did the pilferer believe that strange powers lay within these objects?

This grisly finger is now in the History of Science Museum in Florence, Italy.

HAND OF GLORY

People don't only prize the body parts of the great and the good, but also those of the despicable and the devilish. This is the severed hand of a hanged man. I came across it in Yorkshire, England. But why would anyone keep such an object? Because again, it was said to possess incredible powers.

People believed that if the hand of a hanged man was severed as he still swung from the gallows, the hand would gain the powers to put people to sleep and unlock doors. The perfect tool for a burglar! The thief could even light the fingers of the hand, as if they were candles. If any of the fingers or thumb failed to light, it showed there was someone still awake in the house.

How does this even happen? Opening doors and sending people to sleep? Poppycock.

NOTABLE PEOPLE

When it comes to people, the stranger the better if you ask me, and goodness, I've met some outlandish ones! Perhaps even more curious than the people I've met, are those I've been told about. These three? Unusual, certainly. But they also show how extraordinary the human race is.

GREGOR BACI

Gregor Baci was born in Hungary sometime in the 16th century, and when I visited the country, many there still spoke of him in awe. He was a hussar, a cavalryman who fought on horseback, and he suffered *a truly gruesome accident.* A painting tells us that a lance went straight through an eye and out the other side. Imagine the agony! What's amazing is that Gregor survived and lived for another year. The ends of the lance were sawn off and what remained was left in place while Gregor carried on as normally as he could.

Modern medicine suggests this story could be true. In 2010 a man sustained a similar injury and survived for years afterwards. You could say he was lucky—but perhaps not!

PETRUS GONSALVUS

Petrus Gonsalvus was covered, head to foot, in thick dark hair. I came across his story on the Spanish island of Tenerife, where he was born in 1537. He was treated terribly by his parents, who caged him like a wild animal and fed him raw meat. Then, the French king, Henri II, heard about the child and had his doctor examine him.

He discovered that, despite the hair, Petrus was a boy like any other. The king was kind to Petrus and even got him a teacher so he could learn French and Latin. Petrus went on to marry and have a family.

PETER THE WILD BOY

The German town of Hamelin is famous for the Pied Piper, who's said to have led the town's children away with his magic pipe. But I came across another fascinating story from the same region—that of Peter the Wild Boy.

In 1725 Peter was discovered living in the woods close to the town. He was around twelve years old, and he was naked, walked on all fours, and couldn't talk.

When the King of England, George I, heard of the boy, he had him shipped over to his court as if he were an animal. Once in London the wild boy became a sensation. Newspapers wrote stories about him and a wax model was made of him that the public could visit. But Peter was treated more like a bizarre pet than a human being. If he didn't do as he was told, Peter was beaten.

When King George's royal court became bored of him, Peter was sent to live in the countryside. He was happier there and lived on to become an old man.

Petrus most likely had a very rare medical condition called congenital hypertrichosis. Only around fifty people have had the condition—ever! It's horrifying to think he was caged, but people were much less understanding back then.

Another rare condition. Scientists think Peter had Pitt Hopkins Syndrome which makes learning to speak very difficult. Today, Peter would be more able to get the help and support he deserved, and would not be treated like a pet.

SPIRITUALIS

The spirit realm. Whilst some deny its existence, I believe it's as real as the nose on my face. Often, I've felt the spirits tantalizingly close, only for them to slip away as I reach out, like some will-o-the-wisp. In my mind, this collection of objects is proof the spirits are real.

COMMUNICATING WITH SPIRITS

We humans possess five senses: sight, hearing, smell, taste, and touch. I believe there is a sixth. I can sense when there are spirits among us. When the hairs on the back of my neck prickle I know there is something... out there.

SPIRIT PHOTOGRAPHY

Here, in the late 19th century, photography is all the rage, but these are the most extraordinary pictures I've ever seen. They are photographs of the spirits of dead people: a wife in mourning alongside the ghostly image of her dead husband. A gentleman sitting with the spirit of his wife, long since gone.

They were taken by an American photographer called William Mumler and they've caused a sensation. Across the United States, thousands of people have lost loved ones in the recent Civil War. It's wonderful that these photographs have given people a way to see the dearly departed once again.

No one could tell exactly how Mumler took the photos but, even in his day, many thought he was a fraud. Photography was new technology and some simple camera tricks were enough to fool many people, including Dr. M, into thinking spirits had been captured.

Omnes in eodem
ADAmo participavimus
utque a serpente in
traudem inducti
Sumus, per peccatum
mortui, ac per Coe=
lestem ADAmo
Saluti Restituti
atque ad vitae
lignum, unde
Excideramus
per ignominiae
Lignum reducti.
Sumus.

P. ABAELARDus

SPIRIT WRITING

I love séances, those meetings where we try to communicate with the spirit world through a person called a medium. Spirits communicate in all kinds of ways, from knocking and tapping tables to tipping them over, or making them float in the air. I've seen musical instruments played by ghostly hands and figures materialize in robes that glowed brightly in the dark.

At one particular séance, I was even written a note by something from beyond the grave. *The room lights were dimmed, and the spirits descended.* A sheet of paper, blank before the séance began, was found to be covered in writing once the lights were back on. Incredible.

Most séances had little to do with contacting the dead and most mediums were fraudsters doing simple magician's tricks in the dark. However, many who attended séances were desperate to believe and so were easily convinced.

THE DIVINING PENCIL

Spirit writing isn't new. The Chinese were doing something similar 1,000 years ago. This is a ki pit, or divining pencil, that was used during the Tang Dynasty.

It's a piece of peach wood carved into a two-legged fork with a third, shorter leg, angled down. Two people would each take hold of one leg of the fork, and let the spirits guide them, tracing out characters in sand or ashes with the shorter leg.

It's known as *Fuji writing* and it is still practiced today. People ask the gods for advice on healing sickness, predicting the future, or even finding lost belongings and the ki pit gives them the answer.

WATERLOO TEETH

False teeth have been around for centuries. I've come across sets made from ivory, porcelain, and, believe it or not, even wood. However, the most realistic ones are made of human teeth, but they come at a high price. Thankfully, the wealthy have always been prepared to pay well for a set of human choppers.

However, in the early 1800s you could get human teeth very cheaply, thanks to the Battle of Waterloo.

The conflict, on a single day in June 1815 between the French, British, and Prussians, saw 60,000 soldiers killed. As night fell on the battlefield, scavengers and pickpockets stripped the dead of all valuables—including their teeth.

These teeth made their way to all the grand cities of Europe where dentists offered them as *"Waterloo Teeth."* With so many teeth suddenly available, they became very cheap. And people loved them. They'd rather have young, healthy soldiers' teeth taken after death in battle, than the chops of an old man who had died of some ghastly disease.

I confess I find the idea rather repulsive which is why I'll be giving my ivories an extra brush before bedtime tonight. No false teeth for me.

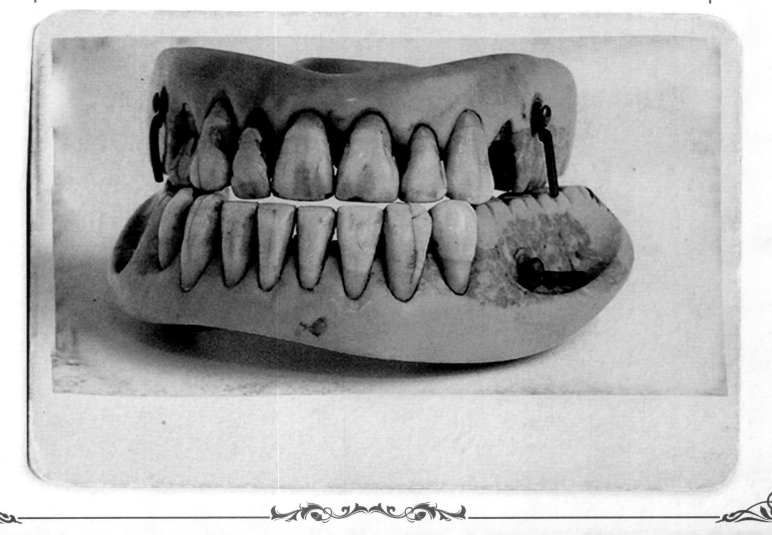

MAGICAE

Magic has been with us since prehistoric times. Witches, shamans, sages, wise ones, call them what you will, but spellcasters are found throughout history, providing curses and incantations designed to bend the forces of nature to our will. Picking through the flotsam and jetsam of witchcraft has unearthed some delightfully disturbing objects.

CASTING SPELLS

Imagine a time before science, when magic ruled and people believed spirits and demons could affect our everyday lives. One sure way to wrestle control from these supernatural beings was with incantations and charms. Believe me, it wasn't just witches that cast spells.

CURSE TABLETS

This curse tablet *dates back over 2,000 years* to Roman times. Made of lead, and beaten as thin as paper with a curse scratched into the metal, curse tablets were rolled up and buried in graves or tombs, nailed to walls of temples, or even thrown into pools of water the way we throw pennies into wishing wells today.

But what did these curses ask for? It turns out, the Romans liked settling scores. Often the curse writer called upon Roman gods such as Charun, Hekate, and Pluto for revenge on their enemies. One writer wished for the person who stole his gloves to go mad and blind. Another wanted a bronze cup that was taken from him to be filled with the blood of the thief.

The writer of this curse was clearly competing in an important chariot race and desperately wanted to win.

I call upon you, o demon, whoever you are, and ask that from this hour, from this day, you torture and kill the horses of the Green and White factions, and that you kill and crush completely the drivers Clarus, Felix, Primulus, and Romanus, and that you leave not a breath in their bodies.

Sadly we've no record as to whether the demon did as he was asked!